T0016947

ALL ABOARD!

TRACTOR

The Farm's Most Amazing Plants, Animals, and Machines

Pavla Hanáčková
Illustrated by Diarmuid Ó Catháin

Sky Pony Press
New York

What's on the menu tonight? Worms, bugs, and berries? Not again! Karl didn't feel like eating the same meal he'd been having for breakfast every night for as long as he could remember. He wanted to try something new, something delicious!

But I don't have the slightest idea where to get new foods. I only know where to find the staples for my pantry!

Karl tried staying up during the day and searching for new foods. Unfortunately, some were out of his reach.

He tried nibbling on a new kind of leaf. Uh oh, that's a kakapo's feather that only resembles a leaf! Mr. Kakapo wasn't very happy about that!

He came across some strange berries, but it didn't feel right to taste them.

Karl sat down; he was tired, and his belly started to rumble.

Then a bee landed on a teeny tiny plant.

Where do plants and other things we eat come from?

That's where goodies come from! I need to find **A FARM!**

HOW TO FARM 101

HOW TO FARM 101

Before we get to work

Karl had never been to a farm before. He quickly realized that growing your own food is no easy matter! There are so many tasks to be done around the farm. How do **farmers** manage to do all of them? They get a lot of work done thanks to their strongest helpers.

Those helpers are in fact farming machines called **tractors**.

The old-fashion way

Have you ever tried planting or harvesting a crop using only your hands and a hoe? It takes a lot of time and energy. In the past, people used **working animals**, such as **oxen** or **horses**, to help them pull carts or plow the fields. But when tractors were invented, it changed farming completely.

Sometimes farming runs in the family. Other times, people decide to become farmers. Either way, they must learn the ropes of farm work.

Farmers need to know their way around different kinds of plants. They learn how to plant them, care for them, and harvest them!

They take the products animals give them—such as milk—and learn to make things we eat out of them. Like cheese!

They must know how to take care of animals, as well. Eve newborns and sick o injured ones!

PARTS OF A TRACTOR

Exhaust pipe

Headlights provide the tractors with plenty of light when working late at night.

Warning lamp

The **cab** is high up and has glass all around, so the driver has a clear view.

The powerful **diesel engine** is not designed for speed, but it enables tractors to pull heavy and big loads.

Mudguards

Big and chunky **tires** can go over any ground and spread the weight of the tractor evenly.

Why are tractors so important?

Since tractors were invented, they have become much more than just a replacement for animals! These powerful machines come in handy in many different situations. They help us trim the trees, clear the snow from roads, dig, or move things around—all thanks to special tools that can be attached to their fronts or backs.

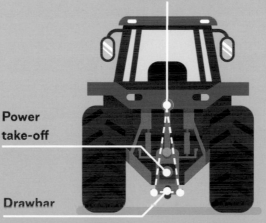

Three-point linkage

Power take-off

Drawbar

How can tractors pull things?

Tractors provide the power, but the **implements** do the work. Trailers, hay balers, or plows can be securely attached to the back of the tractor in three different ways: using a **drawbar**, with a **three-point linkage**, or a **power take-off**.

Super tractors

Tractors were first widely used in the nineteenth century when they replaced oxen, mules, and horses. Do you have an idea what the first tractors looked like? Tractors of today have come a long way from simple engines on wheels. Tractors are amazingly versatile and powerful vehicles that come in all shapes and sizes. Let's have a look at some of the most interesting tractor designs!

Compact tractor

These small tractors are perfect for places with **narrow lanes**, such as vineyards or orchards. The driver can sit high up on them comfortably and pick the fruits or trim the trees at the same time. Very clever!

Row crop tractor

These are the most **versatile** vehicles on the farm. Just add tools to them! Then, they help plant crops in a row, plow, and sow seeds as well as dig holes and move things around! Thanks to the cab, the driver is protected from the heat, dust, and noise.

Tricycle tractor

Designers experimented with design as well as functions. The **John Deere** company came up with a **three-wheeled** tractor. The wheel fitted at the front was great for moving around shorter turns, but tractors were more likely to keel over.

steam engine

solid steel wheels

Steam tractor

The very first tractors were born thanks to **portable steam engines**, which emerged more than one hundred years ago. Later, steel wheels, a driver's seat, and a steering wheel were added to it, and voila! Meet the grandfather of all tractors. Steam tractors were reliable and strong but quite slow.

Crawler tractor

Its oddly shaped wheels are there for a reason. Tough **rubber tracks** don't squash the ground as much as the regular round wheels do; they provide tractors with excellent stability and grip. Sand, snow, or mud—not a problem for crawlers!

driver's cab

rubber tracks

The word *tractor* comes from a Latin word *trahere*, which means "to pull." Makes sense!

Monster tractor

Big Bud 747 is a legendary monster tractor. With its huge tires and a super-duper powerful engine, it can complete even the most demanding of tasks. It was built in the United States more than forty years ago and still boasts the title of the largest farm tractor in the world!

weight over 60 tons

massive tires

Around the farm

Every farm can be divided into several parts. There are buildings where the animals are housed. Some of them have fancy names! Other buildings are used for storing the equipment or harvested crops. And we cannot forget the fields and other places where crops are grown! Let's have a look around!

Barns and pens

Some of these buildings are used as shelters for animals, others are used for storing tools, tractors, and other machinery. See that tall tower next to the barn? That's a **silo**, where grain is stored!

Hay bales

Big bales of dried grass are useful for many reasons: they can be used as feed or bedding for the animals, such as cows, goats, sheep, or horses. Hay is usually stored inside a **barn**, where it's nice and dry.

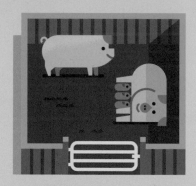

Apiary

Sometimes farmers keep some peculiar animals, such as bees. Why, you ask? Bees are very important, because they are **pollinators**—with their help, many plants and crops can grow.

Chicken coop

Some animals, such as chickens, have special houses to sleep in. Every morning, the farmer lets the chickens out and rushes them back in at dusk. Inside the coop, there are high beams called **roosts**. Chickens like to sleep in higher places. Why? Their ancestors lived in jungles and were safer in the trees. Chickens must remember that!

Farmhouse

Behold! This is the heart of every farm—it's where the farmers live! Farmers often use part of the house as a shop and sell the products they make.

Orchard

Apart from crops, farmers also take care of various groves of trees. Places where farmers keep these fruit or nut trees are called orchards. Look, this farm has an **apple orchard**!

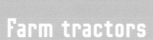

Tractors are one of the most important farm machines!

Farm tractors

Tractors make farmers' lives a lot easier—they move heavy things, speed up the cleaning and feeding processes, and help a great deal in the fields.

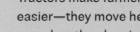

Greenhouse

Why are greenhouses made of glass? During the day, sunlight shines into them and warms the air. Thanks to this trapped, warm air, farmers can grow veggies or flowers inside. Even in winter!

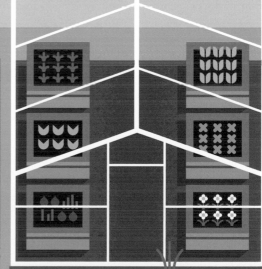

Daily chores on a farm

Farmers get up really, really early (some set their alarms to 5 a.m. and some even earlier). Why, you ask? Because farmers have many chores they must carry out every single day.

Look at these lovely cows! Which steps do farmers need to perform every day to keep the animals happy and healthy? Let's take a peek!

5 Pasture

Animals like being outside, so farmers take them to **pastures** where they can enjoy fresh air and eat some tasty greens. Fences around the pastures keep the farm animals in and unwanted animals out.

6 Rest

The day is almost over! Time to take the animals back to their pens, give them dinner, and let them rest. Look, Karl is so worn out, he took a nap!

4 Feeding

Time for breakfast! Farmers give cows plenty of **water** and **nutritious feed**. This way, cows are healthy and happy!

3 Milking

Time to collect the milk! Cows are **milked** using a special machine, and the milk is then stored.

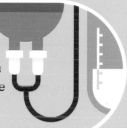

2 New bedding

Farmers replace the old, smelly, and wet bedding with a fresh one. **Hay** or **straw** are usually used as bedding.

1 Cleaning

Just like us, when animals eat, they later produce **waste**. They don't have a special place they can use, so they go to the bathroom in their pens. Farmers therefore clean their pens daily.

Tractors help, too!

Luckily, tractors often lend a helping hand and make everyday chores easier. They can clean the barn in no time, sweeping up the old bedding, tossing it out, and replacing it with a new one. They can even help feed the livestock!

Animals on the farm

Animals play an important part in the farm ecosystem. They eat crops grown on the farm, such as corn and hay. Their waste is also used! Manure is a great fertilizer for the soil. Farmers treat animals with the utmost respect; they want them to be healthy and live happy lives. In return, animals provide many things for people. Let's take a closer look!

Sheep

Sheep like to chomp on grass. They can easily replace a lawn mower! Sheep give us milk, meat, and **wool**. Every year, **sheep-shearing** takes place. Sheep get a haircut and lose about 6.5 pounds of wool, depending on the breed!

wool

mutton

pork

Pigs

Meet one of the smartest and cleanest animals around the farm! Why do they wallow in mud then? To cool down, as pigs don't sweat. Pigs are raised mainly for their **meat** called **pork**. Their skin may be used for **leather**. But some pigs are kept as **pets!**

feathers

poultry

Ducks

These keen swimmers are always near water. Their white **feathers** are very soft! Farmers raise ducks for meat, eggs, and feathers which are used to stuff pillows and comforters.

dairy products

beef

Cows

These black-and-white beauties are raised for meat (called **beef**) or **milk**. Every day, farmers milk their cows and either sell the milk or use it to make their own **dairy products** like cheese, yogurt, or ice cream!

poultry

eggs

You are very welcome to pay me a visit in my forest home!

honey

Bees

The bee family (called a hive) is kept in a special house called an apiary. Each apiary is packed with honeycombs, in which bees live, raise their young, and make **honey** from pollen. The farmers then collect the honey and bottle it up.

Chickens

Chickens are born explorers, and they love to be outside, pecking, digging, and talking to their pals. But they sleep in a special house called a chicken coop. Female chickens, called hens, lay **eggs**. Farmers either collect the eggs or let them hatch.

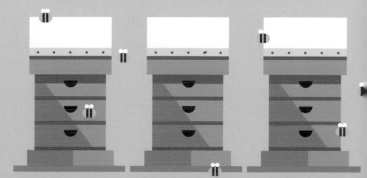

Crops on the farm

The fields and the soil, in which the plants grow, are the heart and soul of every farm. Farmers around the world raise many different crops depending on the climate and culture of their region. All crops have one thing in common: when fully ripe, farmers need to harvest them. Most of the crops, such as vegetables, fruit, and grains like wheat, corn, or rice, make up the food that people eat. They are also used to feed the animals or to make various things out of them.

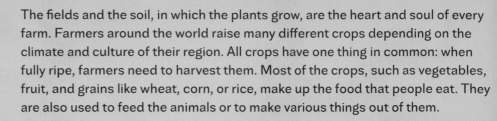

Can you name the most common crops grown all around the world?

cabbage

carrots

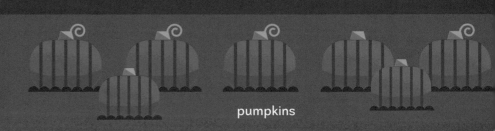

pumpkins

tomatoes

How do plants grow?

Plant a seed in the ground, cover it with soil, and then water it. Soon, something magical will happen! From the tiny seed, a root and sprouts with leaves grow. Leaves fight their way through the soil—they want to see the sun! Under the ground, a surprise awaits: the tiny seed has transformed into a plump radish.

What does a plant need to grow?

sunlight water & air nutrients care

Plants need four basic things to grow: **sunlight, water, air,** and **nutrients**. Plus, care. With their roots, plants absorb water and nutrients from the soil. Plants use every ray of sunshine as the source of their energy—like we do with sleep. From the air, plants "breathe" carbon dioxide and "exhale" oxygen other living creatures need for breathing. This process is called **photosynthesis**.

Wheat

Wheat is one of the most common food crops. Without wheat, there would be no bread, no cakes, no cookies! Wheat is also used for animal feed or even to make fuel.

Corn

Edible yellow seeds are hidden under the husk. Not only can we eat corn, but we make many products from it, be it cooking oils, oil paints, soaps, or even fuel!

Potatoes

Their edible roots are hidden under the ground. Boiled, baked, or fried—a potato is always delicious! No wonder they are a staple food for people all over the world.

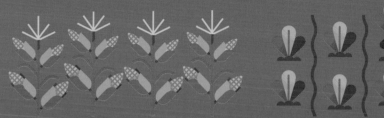

Sunflowers

Sunflowers turn their heads to the sun to catch as many rays of sunshine as possible. We can make oil from sunflowers and eat their seeds!

Rice

Rice is grown in fields or terraced paddies covered with water. About half of the world's population eats rice almost every day!

Cotton

Ready-to-harvest cotton plants have white fluffy tops made of long fibers similar to hair that can be turned into thread we use for making cloth.

What things can we make out of these crops?

Flour is made from wheat or even rice.

Oils are made from corn or sunflower seeds.

French fries are made from potatoes!

Clothes are made from cotton.

Noodles are made from rice or wheat.

Bread is made from wheat.

Harvest time!

Harvest is the busiest time of the year and begins at the end of the summer. Ripe crops must be harvested and stored before winter, so farmers and machines are working in the fields all day long.

Combine harvester

This giant machine helps harvest corn or wheat. With its sharp teeth, it cuts down the wheat and drags it inside the machine, where the grain we eat is separated from the straw. Cleaned grain is stored in the **storage tank**. From the tank, it is unloaded through a **pipe** right into a **trailer**.

Hay baler

Straw is not stored inside the combine harvester; it is tossed on the field, ready for bailing. A **hay baler** collects the straw and makes **hay bales** out of it. The bales then roll out of the back.

Tractors

Tractors collect the hay bales and take them back to the farm. Bales will be stored for winter, used as **bedding** and **feed** for the animals.

Spring

Time to get the fields ready for the new season! Tractors fertilize and plow the fields. With the help of the seed drill, they quickly sow the soil with hundreds of seeds.

Summer

Farmers take care of their crops, making sure they will thrive until the harvest. If needed, they water the crops—or, as a farmer would say, they irrigate them.

Autumn

After the harvest, there is still plenty of work to do. The fields need to be prepped for spring. They are plowed again.

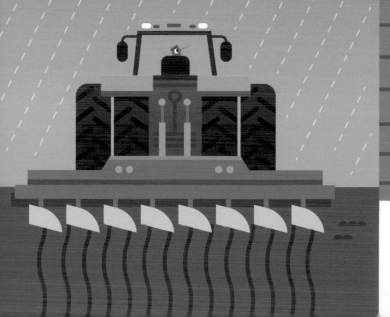

Winter

It's cold and the fields are empty and frozen. Everybody rests. Tractors are parked in the shed, where they are repaired and cleaned.

We can finally unwind after a busy year full of work. But not for too long—spring is around the corner!

Future of farming

Scientists and engineering experts are already working on a new type of tractor: the **autonomous** tractor, or to put it simply, a tractor that drives itself. They would make farmers' lives much easier.

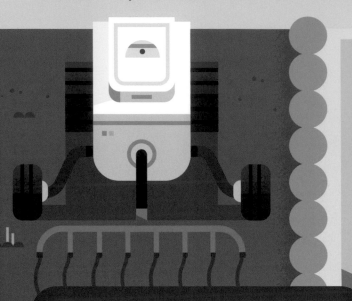

Such tractors will have a computer inside the cab, and farmers will be able to operate them from a distance, using only their phones or tablets.

Not only will these tractors be more efficient and save farmers money and energy, but they will also be more eco-friendly. They will run on electricity generated from solar panels in the fields.

armers will have more time to do some fun activities, like growing the biggest tomato to win a contest . . .

. . . spending more time at farmers' markets and talking to their customers . . .

. . . planting new types of veggies or herbs . . .

. . . cuddling with the animals more . . .

. . . hosting a Carve-a-Pumpkin day at the farm . . .

. . . or holding tractor races!

SOUNDS LIKE A BLAST!

Congratulations!

Look at us! We are real farmers who know the farm and its fields like the back of our hands! Would you like to help me with some chores? All aboard then, and let's do some farming!

Steam tractor

Row crop tractor

Tricycle tractor

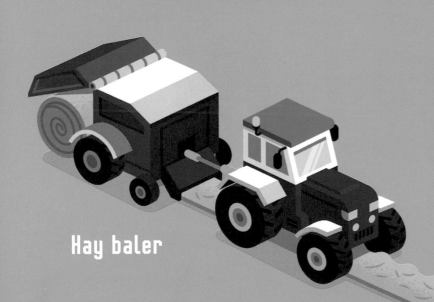

Hay baler

Crawler
tractor

Tractor

Compact
tractor

Monster
tractor

Copyright © 2021 by Pavla Hanáčková
Illustrations copyright © 2021 by Diarmuid Ó Catháin
Published by arrangement with Albatros Media a.s.

First Sky Pony Press edition, 2023

All rights reserved. No part of this book may be reproduced in any manner without the express written consent of the publisher, except in the case of brief excerpts in critical reviews or articles. All inquiries should be addressed to Sky Pony Press, 307 West 36th Street, 11th Floor, New York, NY 10018.

Sky Pony Press books may be purchased in bulk at special discounts for sales promotion, corporate gifts, fund-raising, or educational purposes. Special editions can also be created to specifications. For details, contact the Special Sales Department, Sky Pony Press, 307 West 36th Street, 11th Floor, New York, NY 10018 or info@skyhorsepublishing.com.

Sky Pony® is a registered trademark of Skyhorse Publishing, Inc.®, a Delaware corporation.

Visit our website at www.skyponypress.com.

10 9 8 7 6 5 4 3 2 1

Manufactured in China, September 2022
This product conforms to CPSIA 2008

Library of Congress Cataloging-in-Publication Data is available on file.

Cover design by B4U Publishing, member of Albatros Media Group
Cover illustrations by Diarmuid Ó Catháin
US Edition edited by Nicole Frail

Print ISBN: 978-1-5107-7468-1
Ebook ISBN: 978-1-5107-7469-8